NORWAY

N·W·DAMM&SØN

CONTENTS

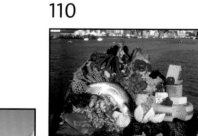

NORWAY - IN A CLASS OF ITS OWN!

Norway's magnificent nature has impressed foreign tourists and Norwegians for generations. Growing environmental awareness in Europe, and elsewhere in the world, has largely resulted in a desire for simple values such as fresh air and pure water. More and more tourists have a desire to experience untouched nature.

Summer in Nusfjord in the Lofoten Islands.

"Back to nature," said French philosophers 200 years ago. "Back to nature," say today's tourists. We have had enough of excess, unnecessary technology and pollution. More and more people are turning towards nature and the gift of virgin wilderness, pure water and clean air.

Generations of Norwegians have made the most of their country and its generous natural resources. Norway has learnt the importance of living in harmony with nature and to protect it against encroachment. Therefore, environmental protection has become a practicable reality in Norway long before it becoming an international issue. It is for this reason that Norway today is a unique land of unsurpassed natural beauty, free to be used by all.

What is unique about Norway, is that you find yourself surrounded by nature wherever you travel in the country. West Norwegians, of course, will claim that the fjords are the most beautiful features in Norway. But how do you compare these to the flowering fruit trees in Hardanger! North Norwegians gesticulate wildly about the beauty of Lofoten and the wonder of the midnight sun, while the people from Trønderlag say that without them Norway would not exist: "What would Norway have been without saint Olav and the Battle of Stiklestad? And so the argument continues ad infinitum!

Norway has a rich tradition in art and crafts; shown in exotic silver jewellery from Vikings times and in colourful national costumes. There is also a long tradition in using old patterns in modern knitwear design, and beautiful wood carvings and ornamental knives are also part of Norwegian folklore.

Sami art and crafts are particularly attractive and colourful. The Sami produce a broad selection of knives, clothes, knitted jackets, hats, shoes and unusual products made from reindeer hide.

Then there is food. Certain Norwegian specialities are a must for the tourist. When in season, sweet Norwegian strawberries cannot be beaten. Norwegians adore thick slices of goats' milk cheese on bread. It may sound unappetizing to the visitor, but you will seldom find a breakfast table laid without this unique-tasting speciality. For a snack, you can chew a piece of fresh dried cod. It tastes of the sea, the wind and the Arctic summer!

Norway has also become the stage for a host of historical and cultural events. There are the saga plays in Trøndelag, the Molde jazz festival, celebrations in Bergen and the Ibsen festival in Grimstad to name but a few.

Come and join the adventure!

OSLO AND THE OSLO FJORD

Færder lighthouse marks the entrance to the Oslo fjord. The fjord represents one of the most beautiful introductions to a capital city that you could ever experience. Passenger ferries from continental Europe gracefully enter the fjord surrounded by a sea of white sails. Boating and fishing are a way of life for Norwegians. Yachts, cabin cruisers and cobbles bob gently as fresh fish and steaks are grilled on board.

HISTORY

The area around the Oslo fjord is scattered with ancient relics from the past. The Oseberg ship and other famous Viking remains were found here, and the Fredriksten fort in Halden bears witness to the fact that Norway has not always been at peace with Sweden.

OSLO

Oslo is full of restaurants, discotheques, night clubs, noisy outdoor venues and intimate cafes. Uniquely positioned between mountains and fjord, its numerous museums, commercial enterprises, parks and activities, make Oslo an unforgettable place to spend a holiday.

SURROUNDING AREA

Less than an hour from the centre of Oslo, you can stroll through endless pine forests, sunbathe on a beach, climb mountains, visit rich farming country, or go scuba diving and sea fishing.

ATTRACTIONS

Hardly anywhere else in the country can boast as many fascinating museums as can the Oslo region. Vigeland Park and the Fram, Kon-Tiki and Viking Ship museums are a must for everyone visiting the capital. In addition, there is the famous Munch Museum at Tøyen, the neighbouring botanical gardens, a science and technology museum, the Skiing museum at Holmekollen and many other places of interest. The old town in Fredrikstad and Fredriksten fort in Halden

Oslo harbour and the City Hall.

are but two of the many interesting places worth a visit in Østfold. Places of interest on the west side of the fjord include Slottsfjellet in Tønsberg and Blaafarveværket at Modum.

Holmenkollen ski-jump with the Oslo fjord in the background.

King Harald V, Queen Sonja, Crown Prince Haakon Magnus, Crown Princess Mette-Marit and Princess Ingrid Alexandra.

The Norwegian
parliament,
the Storting.

Akershus Fort
built around
1300 A.D.

Vigeland Park
The park contains the world's largest collection of sculptures created by one man, Gustav Vigeland (1869-1943).
They portray man's existence on earth. The collection comprises 192 sculptures, totalling 650 figures.

Traditional Folk
Dancing at the
Folk Museum
in Oslo.

Edvard Munch's famous painting, "The Scream".

Fram, the vessel built for Fridtjof
Nansen's Polar expedition.

The Viking Ship Museum
The museum houses ships
and relics from the Viking
times.

The Kon-Tiki Museum houses
the original balsa raft that sailed across the Pacific Ocean
from Peru to Polynesia in
1947, and the papyrus boat,
RA II, which sailed across the
Atlantic from Morocco to
Barbados in 1970.

Oslo is noted for its idyllic surroundings.

SOUTH NORWAY
AND TELEMARK

One mention of "Sørlandet" (South Norway) and every Norwegian dreams about white beaches, rocky islets, seagulls, ripe strawberries, the sea and fishing: in short, summer holidays!

But not many know that South Norway, Setesdal and Telemark can also offer a relaxing atmosphere and a multitude of exciting activities throughout the year!

SKERRIES
The skerries off the South Norwegian coast are one of the most unusual offshore rock formations in Europe, north of Egeerhavet. There are an untold number of rocky islets and deserted beaches here; with a boat you can sail to wherever the wind takes you!

TRADITIONAL HOUSES
The whitewashed houses, bedecked in roses, are typical of the region. In Telemark and Setesdal, 800-year-old storehouses resting on stone pillars are fine examples of Norway's policy of preserving quality and tradition for posterity. The island community of Lyngør was chosen as Europe's best-kept community in 1990!

Heddal stave church is Norway's oldest and best preserved.

MOUNTAINS AND VALLEYS
Inland, the region has another story to tell. Pleasant country roads offer numerous opportunities to study local culture and history. Take a detour off the beaten track and you will find well stocked fishing lakes and beautiful countryside to calm the soul and leave you rejuvenated. Here, you can search after rare minerals and precious stones in disused mines, go canoeing, horse-riding or even join a beaver safari. In addition, there is the unique journey along the 100-year-old Telemark canal aboard the M/S Victoria from Skien. The canal is a monument to man's ingenuity, with manual locks raising the "Victoria" and "Henrik Ibsen" 72 m and 110 km inland to the foothills of the mountain range.

Idyllic Ulvøysund.

In Setesdal and upper Telemark, traditional folk culture is expressed in music and improvised poetry, in regional costume, silversmithing and other handicrafts.

CHILDREN
The region is a paradise for children. You can visit the children's theme park "Kardemommeby" and the Animal Park. There are several water parks such as Sommerland in Telemark; as well as working farms, boating, beaches and crab fishing.

The Lyngor island community.

South Norway is a paradise for children.

Kardemommeby Theme Park
near Kristiansand.

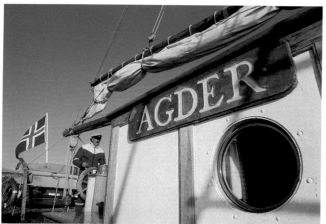

Lindesnes lighthouse.

Living room in Telemark decorated with traditional floral motif.

Carving from the 17th century.

Over a 200-year period in the Middle Ages, around 1,200 churches were built in Norway. Thirty of these are still standing. Heddal stave church is one of the largest.

Winter sunset in Jotunheim

TROLL PARK AND THE NORWEGIAN MOUNTAINS

*Norwegian folklore origi-
nated in the region stretching west-east from
Hardangervidda to the
Swedish border: an area
abound with pixies,
wood nymphs and trolls.*

*The rock you rest on
may appear to be stone,
but who knows, it could
be the remains of the
troll king who turned
into stone at sunrise!*

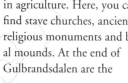

MOUNTAINS

Few countries can boast so much virgin nature as Norway. The region stretching from the watershed in the West to the border region in the East has become known as the Troll Park, and includes Hardangervidda, the Hemsedal mountains, Valdres, Gulbrandsdalen and Østerdalen. This area offers enormous opportunities for recreation designed to stimulate senses and exercise muscles. The Norwegian mountains offer challenges to anglers, skiers, mountain climbers, hikers and hunters alike.

VALLEYS

Guldrandsdalen is a broad fertile valley with a long tradition in agriculture. Here, you can find stave churches, ancient religious monuments and burial mounds. At the end of Gulbrandsdalen are the Rondane mountains, a little to the west is situated Jotuheimen, Norway's highest mountain range and perhaps most famous national park.

A quarter of Norway's unique stave churches is found at Valdres, along with many of the country's best fishing lakes. Hallingdal is home to some of the best sports centres in Norway such as Hemsedal, Geilo and Gol. Østerdalen is covered in forest, but if you really want to "get away from it all", take a canoe trip on Femundsjøen.

LIFE AFTER THE OLYMPICS

Lillehammer and the area around Mjøsa (Norway's longest lake) have much to offer tourists visiting the site of the 1994 Winter Olympics. These include the Viking Ship stadium at Hamar and Fjellhallen, the stadium built in a mountain at Gjøvik. You cannot visit Lillehammer without viewing the Sandvigske historical collection near Maihaugen. Folklore and trolls are the theme of Hunderfossen Family Park, just north of the town.

Norway's mountains are breathtaking.

Besseggen in Jotunheimen. →

ACTIVITIES

The magnificent countryside offers activities to suit all tastes. Here are just a few examples: mountain climbing and horseriding in Hemsedal; hiking and jogging over Hardangervidda; trout fishing in Mjøsa or white-water rafting at Sjoa. For the less active, there is traditional glass blowing at the famous Hadeland Glass Factory.

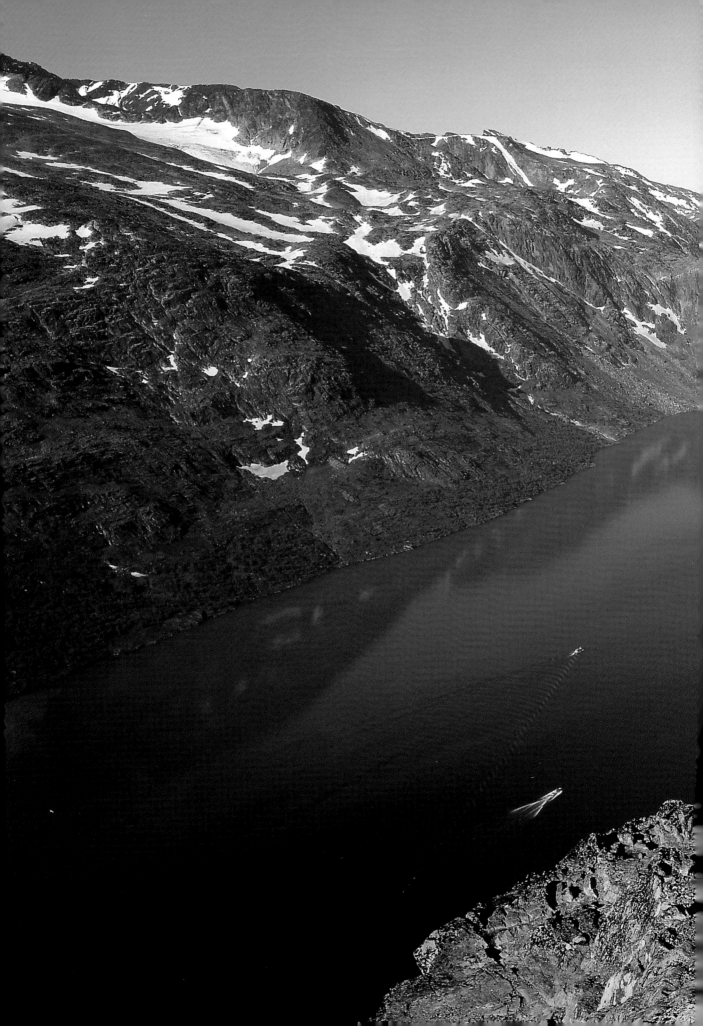

Reindeer in
Jotunheim

Rafting on the River Sjoa.

Hiking in Rausdalen.

35

Hunting, fishing and enjoying the nature.

Bear and a family of elk.

Mountain farm.

The Skibladner on Mjøsa, Norway's largest lake. A trip on the world's oldest operational paddle steamer should not be missed.

The Sandvigske collection at Maihaugen in Lillehammer is one of North Europe's most exciting
open-air museums. It contains 150 historical buildings.

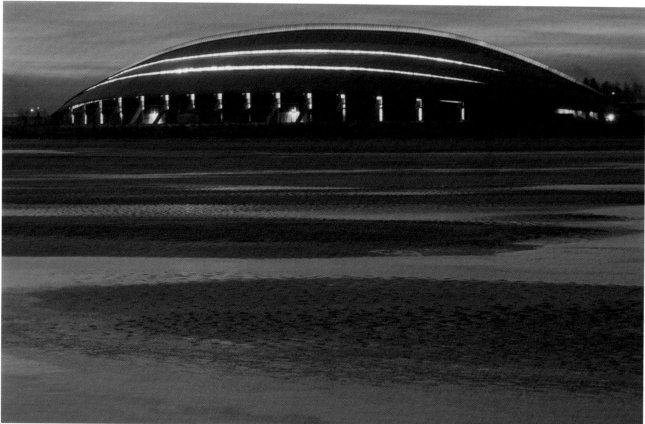

The 17th Winter Olympic Games were held in the Lillehammer region.

←← The Viking Ship - Olympic ice skating arena in Hamar.

← Winter at Vang in Valdres.

The ruins of the Medieval Cathedral in Hamar are now preserved under a beautiful structure of glass and steel.

Experience Norway in the winter.

CENTRAL NORWAY

A Trøndelag saying goes something like this: "Take Trøndelag out of the history books and only the covers will remain." This may seem an exaggeration but Norwegian kings of yore came to Frosta for final "approval", and in more recent times, kings have been accepted in Nidaros Cathedral.

Musk on Dovrefjell

HISTORY

Trøndelag has more ancient rock carvings than any other county in Norway. In 1030, saint Olav fell at Stiklestad in Verdalen, thus giving it a permanent place in history. Trondheim was the capital and seat of the Archbishop. Nidaros Cathedral, Scandinavia's largest structure from the Middle Ages, was the Coronation Church for several hundred years and the Norwegian Crown Jewels can still be viewed there.

NATURE

Trøndelag is a paradise for nature lovers. The county has everything to offer from a sandy Atlantic coastline to virgin wilderness. It is worth spending several days at the Dovrefjell, Gressåmoen and Børgefjell national parks.

FISHING

Orkla, Gaula, Stordalselva, Stjørdalselva and Verdalselva are widely known as excellent salmon rivers. In the "queen" of the salmon rivers, the Namsen, anglers landed more than 33,000 kilos in 1990! If you want to try your hand all you need is luck - both equipment and guides are available for hire. Fantastic skerries and numerous lakes also offer good fishing prospects, as does the ocean. The sea fishing season starts in March/April!

TOWN AND VILLAGE

Trondheim has all the advantages of a city combined with small-town charm. Moreover, Trondheimsfjorden offers many pleasurable activities. Steinkjer has numerous burial grounds from the Viking period, whilst Oppdal is the gateway to the Dovrefjell National Park.

Røros is definitely worth a visit. The unique timber buildings of this mining town are on UNESCO's list of 300 cultural treasures most worthy of protection in the world!

EXPERIENCES

No imagination is needed to find exciting things to do in Central Norway. Nature and culture are there for the taking.

NAMSOS

STEINKJER

TRONDHEIM

OPPDAL   RØROS

The magnificent church at Røros and the enormous slag heaps from over 300 years of mining.

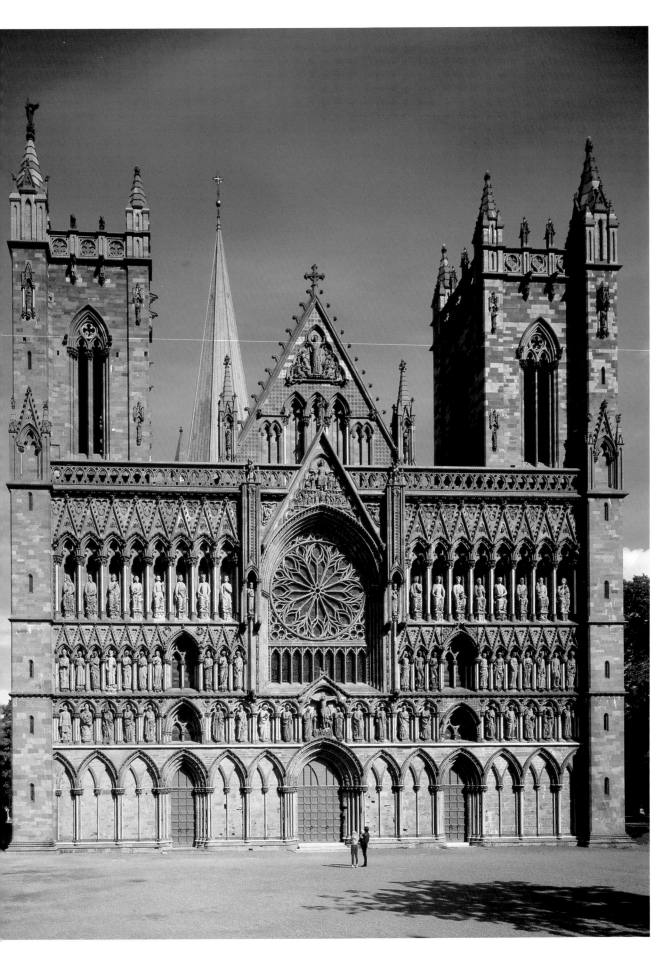

The queen of Norwegian churches - Nidaros Cathedral in Trondheim.

Reindeer at dusk.

Norway is an eldorado for anglers.

A Norwegian fjord extends and unfolds like a gigantic picture postcard.

FJORDS AND MOUNTAINS

The fjords of West Norway are perhaps the country's most striking image, famous the world over. This, of course, comes as no surprise to anyone who has sailed up Nærøyfjorden on a still, spring morning, with soaring snow-capped mountain peaks as a backdrop. The view of the "seven sisters" rising majestically from the depths of Geirangerfjorden as the Friarfoss waterfall tumbles perpetually downwards is unforgettable.

GLACIERS

Standing at the bottom of a million-year-old glacier is simply awe-inspiring. The freezing mass, grey-white with age, plunges downwards towards the turquoise fjord.
The water streaming out of the glacier is never warmer than 2°C. With an experienced guide, you can visit the foot of the glacier or go skiing between frightening crevasses. The Jostedal glacier in Sogn and Fjordane is the largest land-based glacier in Europe. You can study the amazing history of this geological wonder at the new glacier museum in Fjærland.

STOREHOUSES AND STAVE CHURCHES

Architecture in West Norway is as varied as it is unique. The old quays in Bergen are colourful reminders of the Hanseatic trade of the early eighteenth century, and the tarred stave churches are the only ones of their type in the world. Handsome Swiss-style hotels built before the turn of the century offer a warm welcome throughout the region. In Ålesund, you can admire the Jugendstil architecture from the quayside.

FLOWERING FRUIT TREES

West Norway offers many incomparable experiences. The flowering fruit trees in Hardanger are perhaps one of the most beautiful sights you will ever see in your life, while the annual celebrations in Fjordane is the largest land-based glacier in Europe. You can study the amazing history of this geological wonder at the new glacier museum in Fjærland.

Ferryboat and blossoming fruit trees in Kaupanger.

Geiranger - an experience!

Bergen and the Molde jazz festival are cultural events that attract attention the world over.

The Vøringsfoss waterfall and the Lysefjord road, with its 28 hairpin bends, are two more examples of the diversity of this region. Have you ever been skiing in July? At Strynefjellet, you can hire both skis and shorts!

Borgund stave church in Lærdal.

← Aurlandsfjorden - a magnificent area of Sognefjorden.

Lovannet, inner Nordfjord.

Urnes stave church in Luster is the oldest in Norway.

View over
Jostedalen.

Jølster

← The Briksdal glacier, Nordfjord.

Summer skiing at Strynsfjellet.

Dramatic surroundings on the Nigard
glacier ↑→

Majestic Prekestolen rises 600 m above the fjord.

← The Flåm railway is the most exciting railway journey in Scandinavia.

Red daybreak at Kvassheim in Jæren.

Just after sunset at Mølen in Vestfold.

The Buer
glacier.

Låtefoss

The Hardanger landscape is
full of contrasts.

Steindalsfossen

Vøringsfossen is 183 m high.

↑ → Kjeåsen mountain farm in Eidfjord, Hardanger. The region is rich in culture and tradition. Norway's national instrument, the fiddle, originated here.

← Spring in Hardanger.

Vang church in Voss was built in 1277 A.D.

Agatun

The Barony Rosendal in Kvinnherad is an unusual relic from 1665.

BERGEN - GATEWAY TO FJORD COUNTRY

Bergen is the capital of West Norway and the gateway to wonderful fjords. It is Scandinavia's greatest tourist attraction. Whether you arrive by car, bus, boat, train or air, the journey itself is an experience.

The city is a peculiar mix. It is cosy and intimate, while at the same time venerable and international. In fact, Bergen is so international that many of its citizens regard it as a separate state: "We're not from Norway, we're from Bergen," say the inhabitants with a wry smile. And they'll say it to any stranger they meet, for Bergensians are noted for their openness and friendly nature, despite coming from a community hemmed in by mountains. With its natural harbour connected to the North Sea, Bergen grew as an important international port on the Hanseatic trade route between Europe and Northern Russia. Today, Bergen is also an important fishing port. The centre comprises the harbour and the old quays and, to first-time visitors at least, it seems that all important decisions are taken at the fish market.

"Bryggen"

→ ↗ Troldhaugen, Bergen - the home of the Norwegian composer Edvard Grieg.

Bergen Aquarium.

The famous fish market in Bergen.

The Fløyen and Ulriken offer a fantastic view over Bergen.

Bergen →

Dramatic Trollveggen in Romsdal.

Hair-raising journey down Trollstigveien in Romsdal.

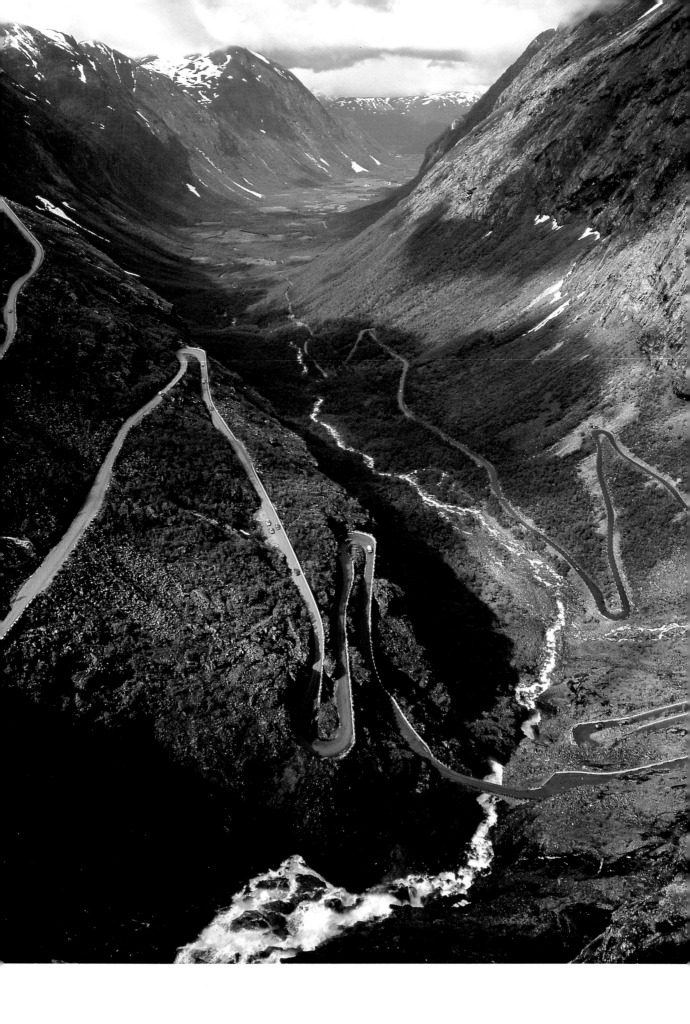

WHAT IS A FJORD?

Many Norwegian fjords stretch over 200 kilometres inland. They can be as deep as the surrounding mountains are high. Depths of up to 1,300 metres have been recorded, though at the entrance of a fjord, the water is much shallower, sometimes only 10-20 meters deep. The fjords were originally valleys caused by river erosion. During successive ice ages, enormous glaciers widened and lengthened the valleys. The glaciers gouged out the valley profile and pushed ahead of it boulders and massive rock, which where eventually deposited where the glacier met the sea. Roughly 10-20,000 years ago the glaciers retreated. Settlers followed and soon realized they had stumbled across a new Eden: for the coast of Norway and the fjords were nourished by the warm currents of the Gulf Stream, which produced a far milder climate than other regions on the same latitude.

View over Geiranger.

A natural bridal veil →

↑↑ Runde at Ålesund is Norway's highest nesting cliff. ↑ Puffins.

Diving off a wreck near Sula in Møre og Romsdal.

Atlanterhavsveien - selected the construction of the century.

Ålesund - a beautiful town situated on three islands. →

NORTH NORWAY

The wonderful wild nature of North Norway will leave you spell-bound. The mountains, ocean, plains and fjords are so fantastic that they are guaranteed to take the breath of even the most experienced traveller.

Here and there are remote fishing stations, hidden gems waiting to be discovered.

Hamnøy in Lofoten.

Hurtigruten - the most beautiful sea voyage in the world ➔

PEOPLE

North Norwegians are renowned for their openness; an openness that is as genuine as the Arctic Ocean is deep. Their friendliness is in stark contrast to the brutal nature that surrounds them. The midnight sun is used as an alibi for holding cheerful get-togethers and lively discussions well into the early hours of the morning.

GETTING THERE

The best way to visit the three northernmost counties is by boat. The coastal express service, also known as "national route one", represents one of the world's most beautiful sea journeys. In a shifting breeze, the fairy tale coast appears a subtle shade of blue, while the world's oldest mountains at Lofot rise majestically to present a seemingly impenetrable wall. When the ship departs for all points north, you can take your time and visit the rest of the region by road.

NATURE

The ocean, mountains and plains are basic elements of the wild nature of North Norway. Finnmarksvidda alone can boast 60,000 fishing lakes and thousands of kilometres of salmon and trout rivers. Divers from all over the world meet here to experience the crystal clear waters that wash the myriad of islands, islets and skerries. Birdlife knows no bounds, and for mountain climbers, hikers and skiers, the raw landscape presents new challenges. Winter fishing off the Lofoten islands is an international top-level event. The coast of North Norway has always been noted as one of the richest fishing zones in the world. Lofoten was a centre of power in Viking times. The largest Viking building ever found, was discovered at "Borg" in Lofoten.

CITIES

But Europe's "summit" has definitely more to offer than fantastic nature. The city of

Tromsø has been accurately described as the "Paris of the North": teeming with restaurants, bars, night clubs and cafes. Harstad is famous for hosting the North Norwegian folk festival each summer. Otherwise, all the towns and villages of the region hold festivals or celebrations sometime during the year.

EXPERIENCES

Whether you spend your time by the ocean or in the country, North Norway guarantees you a memorable experience. But don't think North Norway is all about sports and activities.

If you're looking for a quiet holiday take our advice and try a traditional fishermen's cabin in Lofoten, where the fish bite right outside your doorstep!

Beautiful Kjerringøy with the old trading centre, north of Bodø.

A fairy-tale coastline.

The Arctic Circle
Centre - the most
popular attraction
in North Norway.

Saltstraumen
near Bodø is the
world's most
powerful whirlpool.

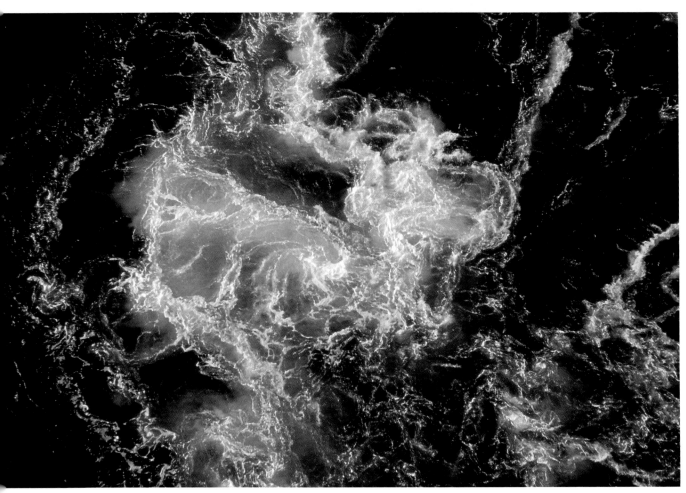

Tromsø, the "Paris of the North".

Reine in Lofoten - defies description. →

Henningsvær - picturesque Lofoten is unforgettable.

Not a catch, but a meal fit for a king.

↑↑ Træna - Norway's oldest fishing station.

Haukelandstrand, Lofoten

↑↑ Summer at Torghatten in Nordland.

Rock carvings at Alta - the designer died more than 3,000 years ago!

Finnmark is the centre for Sami culture. →

Sunset at North Cape -
the northernmost tip of
Europe.

SVALBARD – EXOTIC, WILD AND BEAUTIFUL

Do you dream about going somewhere different for your holidays? Do you need to get away from the hustle and bustle of city life? Have you a desire to get back to nature? Are you looking for an exciting active holiday or simply peace and quiet? If your answer is yes to any of these, then travel to Svalbard, a unique part of Norway situated far north in the Arctic Ocean.

SVALBARD LIGHT

During the summer, Svalbard is bathed in sunlight 24 hours a day. In the winter, the ice-bound and snow covered Arctic islands rely on shimmering stars, moonlight and the aurora borealis for light. Arctic nights on Svalbard can be indescribably beautiful.

SVALBARD IS AN ARCTIC WILDERNESS

The thousands of square kilometres of mountains, fjords, valleys and glacier that make up Svalbard can appear inhospitable at first sight. However, Svalbard has been populated for centuries and there are numerous signs to prove it. Hunters, explorers and adventurers have all found their way to this northern archipelago. The population today is mainly concentrated on the largest of the islands, Spitsbergen; either in the principal Norwegian community of Longyearbyen or at the two Russian settlements of Barentsburg and Pyramiden.

SVALBARD HAS NO BORDERS

Svalbard has neither borders nor a passport control. All visitors are welcome. You are also welcome to experience the wilderness. Despite great distances and fickle Arctic weather, modern transport facilities and well-organized travel guides make it possible to tour the islands relatively easily - even though there aren't any roads!

SVALBARD IS DIFFERENT

The Arctic landscape is unique and extremely vulnerable. The climate presents extremely difficult conditions for the indigenous plant and animal life of the region. All travel and activities on Svalbard take account of the fact that the environment has to be protected. Visitors must also be aware of the need to protect the natural environment here. Take care of Svalbard!

SVALBARD HAS MUCH TO OFFER

Stay at Longyearbyen and you experience a living mining community. The town offers all kinds of facilities and things to do. You can take a boat trip, perhaps combined with a tour on foot. You can visit other settlements either by boat, snow scooter or aeroplane. Otherwise you can cross the Arctic expanse by dog sledge, on skis or by foot. The choice is yours!

HISTORY OF THE TROLLS

Far to the North where the winter storms whip the weather-beaten coasts, you will find a long and narrow country. Here you see dark forests with moonlit lakes, deep fjords surrounded by mighty snowcapped mountains, and long rivers and cold streams cascading down the mountain sides.

Nowadays this country is covered by snow and ice only six months a year. A long, long time ago, however, there existed a massive glacier that brooded over the entire country for thousands of years.

As the climate gradually warmed and the glacier slowly retreated to the North, Man to the South of the glacier followed in its wake. Looking at this country and finding it to be magnificent, they considered themselves to be its first inhabitants. People settled there and named it Norway. They were themselves called 'nordmenn' (Men of the North).

It did not take them long, however, to realize that on this land there were various other creatures hiding out in the forests and mountain sides. People did not know what these creatures were, but they were generally believed to have supernatural powers, and they came to be known as trolls.

The trolls would come out of their hiding-places only after sun-set, and they would disappear before the mor-

ning sun arose in the East. Direct exposure to the sun could cause them to crack, turn into stone and possibly burst. On occasion the trolls would evidently forget to hide from the sun, and rock formations can today be found in various places with troll-like features.

The trolls were mostly seen on bright moonlit nights, or during stormy nights that

farmers sons, who were lured to the mountains by these fairies, would usually check for tails on their new-found beauties.

The wrath of the trolls was boundless. It was therefore considered very important not to make them your enemy. If a farmer did provoke a troll, his livestock might be subject to disease or harmful sickness, or worse things could happen. On the other hand, a good relationship with the trolls could be very rewarding.

Now, even in modern times it is well advised to keep a good standing with the trolls, since you never know when you will meet one yourself. The next time you go to the dark forests and the mighty mountains with their deep lakes and roaring waterfalls, just remember, they probably mean no harm. But be aware. In the twilight hours you are no longer alone.

Then it is only you . . . and all the trolls.

---

could frighten about anyone who happened to be outdoors at that time.

The trolls had very distinct features. They had long crooked noses, only four fingers and toes on each limb, and most of them had long bushy tails.

Some trolls were giants, and others were small. There were stories of two-headed as well as three-headed trolls, and even a few had only one eye in the middle of their wrinkled foreheads. Others had trees and rough moss-like growth all over their heads and noses.

Although they were shaggy and rough-haired, and most looked frightening, they were also known to be good-natured and naive. So naive in fact that even sly peasant boys could, on occasion, easily trick them. Stories about such encounters are common in the fairy tales.

Most trolls lived to be hundreds of years old. However, because of the trolls extremely shy nature, their true origin, their lifestyle or what surprises they might pull has always been a mystery.

The ability to transform themselves counted among the

trolls many supernatural skills. The fairy maidens – called "Hulder" – could transform into incredibly attractive young ladies. However, they could not get rid of their tails. Hunters and

THE NORWEGIAN CUISINE

The history of the Norwegian cooking goes back a long way. It is closely connected to natural resources found in Norway: freshwater fish, saltwater fish, game from the forests and mountains and grain, milk and meat from one of the most marginal agricultural industries in Europe. Of course, the menu has changed and developed through the ages, influenced by economic improvement, changing climate and international influence. But although the "pizza" is often regarded as Norway's national dish, the true Norwegian kitchen remains based on traditional raw materials and customs.

BUFFET LUNCH

A Norwegian buffet lunch is a culinary experience. The table simply overflows with delicious food. A typical buffet will include inter alia:

- a selection of breads
- different types of milk and juices
- diverse salads with various dressings
- several types of herring
- shellfish and fish prepared in various ways
- an assortment of sliced meats
- various cured meats and garnishes
- hot courses of fish and meat, sometimes pasta
- an abundance of cheese and fruit
- desserts including creamed rice, caramel and chocolate pudding, souffles, cakes, wild berries and fresh fruits.

A Norwegian buffet is a fantastic sight. The food is presented without being covered in sauce or aspic; the taste is in the food itself.

MUTTON AND CABBAGE STEW

In September, the sun hangs low in the sky and golden trees cast long shadows. It is time for entertaining indoors around a roaring fire - it is time for mutton and cabbage stew. This is a simple traditional country dish eaten throughout Norway. The autumnal company around a steaming stewpot says much about Norwegian eating habits. Not only is this genial stew a favourite of all Norwegians, but it also involves getting together around the table for a communal meal. To congregate around the dining table, in each other's houses, is an important aspect of Norwegian food culture.

10-12 portions
3 kg mutton
3 kg cabbage
salt
1 tbsp whole black pepper
1 litre boiling water
90 g plain flour

Chop meat from the shoulder, ribs, neck or back into servings and place in alternate layers with roughly chopped cabbage in a large pot. Add salt and pepper to each layer. Add boiling water and boil again. Let it simmer until the meat has turned dark (approx. 1 hour 30 minutes). Add salt and pepper to taste. It should be quite peppery. Stir the flour in a little water and carefully pour this over the stew, stirring all the time, until the gravy is smooth. Boil again. Serve with boiled potatoes.

FISH GALORE!

Fish has always held a special place in the Norwegian kitchen. The Norwegian coast is characterized by mountains, fjords and a small, narrow strip of cultivable soil. The farms along the coast have in general been too small and unproduc-

PINNEKJØTT – Christmas dish from the West Coast of Norway. Salted mutton rib served with boiled potatoes and mashed yellow turnip.

tive to support a family alone.
Most have had to resort to
fishing as their main source
of income.

Fish as a main meal 2-3 times
a week is still usual among a
large portion of the
population. The coastal waters
of Norway contain some of
the richest fish resources in the
world. Therefore, it is not sur-
prising that fish has had a grea-
ter influence in the develop-
ment of the Norway kitchen
than in many other countries.

COLD COOKED
SALMON.

Cold cooked fish is a delicacy
in the summer. The fish is prepared some hours before ser-
ving. All the ingredients except
the potatoes can be prepared
beforehand without losing any
of the quality.

180 g of cooked salmon fillet
per person
0.5 dl sour cream
1 ts lemon juice
sugar
or
0.5 dl full cream

horseradish
1 ts 7% vinegar
sugar

The fish should preferably be
free of skin and bones.
Whip the sour cream and add
lemon juice and sugar to taste
or
whip the full cream until it is
thin and add grated horseradish, vinegar and sugar to taste. The cream thickens quickly
when ingredients are added so
do not over-stir.
Make a cucumber or lettuce
salad with a vinegar or
oil/vinegar dressing.
Serve with boiled potatoes.

LUTEFISK (DRIED
CODFISH PREPARED IN
POTASH LYE)

The characteristic smell of
lutefisk pervades all Norwegian
fish restaurants at Christmas.
In the last week before
Christmas, the most popular
fish restaurants of Oslo are
packed solid with Norwegians
eating lutefisk. For some reason, the coldest and darkest
month is the season for eating
this unusual dish.

When passionate lutefisk-
lovers gather round the table,
they are preparing for a culinary feast.

Originally, the dried fish was
soaked in lye made from ash
from a birch tree, but today
caustic soda is used.
The fish is soaked in lye for 2-
3 days, until it is tender (when
a finger can be pressed into the
fillet without much resistance).
It is then left under running
water for a couple of days,
until all caustic soda is washed
out.

750 g lutefisk per person
water
salt, 0.5 dl salt per litre water

Cut the fish into sizeable portions and place in cold water for
30 minutes before boiling.
Place the lutefisk directly into
boiling salted water. Boil again
and remove from the heat.

Scrape off the scum from the
surface of the water and allow
the fish to stand for 5-10
minutes.

Lutefisk is served with bacon
fat, mushy peas, boiled potatoes, butter, mustard sauce,
flat bread or traditional "lefse".

NATIONAL COSTUMES
- AN IMPORTANT ELEMENT OF NORWEGIAN CULTURE.

Norwegians are extremely proud of their national costumes or "bunads". There is a strong tradition in Norway for dressing for the right occasion and there is a clear distinction between national dress and national costumes.

National dress describes everyday wear. Everything from work clothes to clothes used for festivals and special occasions. Early Norwegians were very particular about dressing correctly. The finest clothes were always worn to church. Researchers say it is this tradition that continues in present day national costumes.

NATIONAL COSTUMES, as defined here, first appeared about 100 years ago. At the end of the nineteenth century, when national dress was becoming less popular, a wave of national romanticism hit Norway. Thus, national costumes were based on latter-day national dress.

It is becoming increasingly popular to wear national costu-

National costume of husband and wife from Voss.

mes for special occasions. With their wide variation (they differ from region to region) and active role in present day fashion, national costumes are an important pillar in Norwegian folklore. One of the reasons for this extensive interest in national costumes is that Norwegians have a desire to find their roots. There is a popular desire for creating things that are durable, beautiful and pure-Norwegian.

National costume from Nordland.

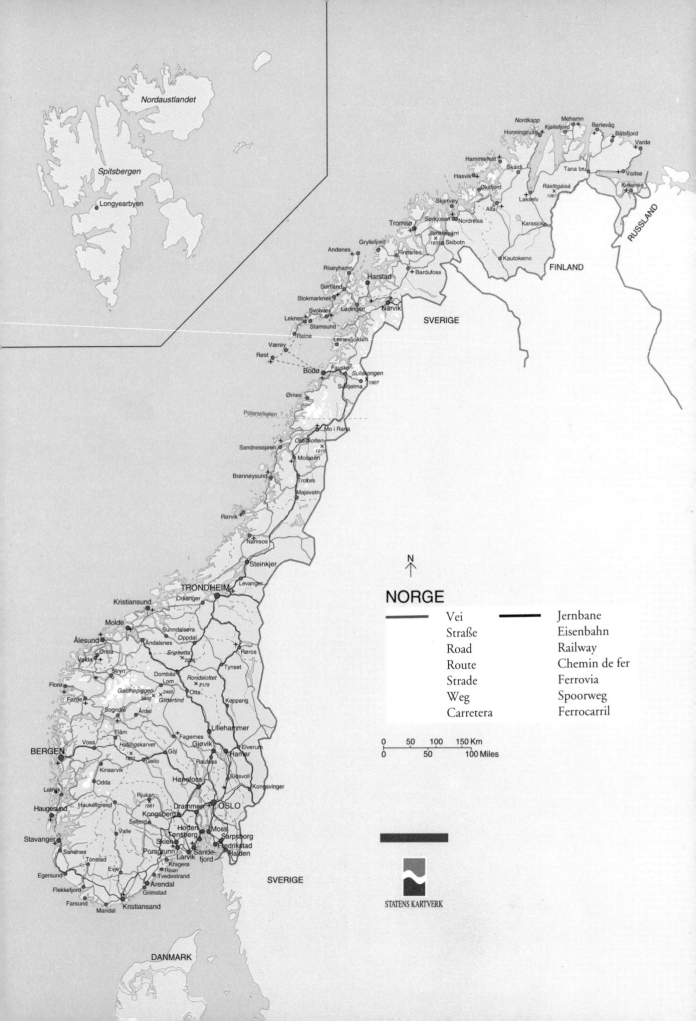

© N.W. Damm & Søn AS
N-0055 OSLO

This book is published in cooperation with Bergen tourist board
Printing: Narayana Press, Denmark
12. printing 2006

Picture sources: Samfoto Husmofoto, To-foto, The Image Bank
Kristiansen, Paulstad, Bård Løken, Bjørn Schulze, Thomas Barstad, Scanpix.
Tourist information: Nortra.
History of the trolls source material: Trygve Torgersen.
National costumes source material: 'Norges bunader og samiske folke-
drakter' by Heidi Fossnes, published by JW Cappelen.
Norwegian cuisine source material: 'Vårt norske kjøkken' by Sven Gran.
Published by Kom forlag.
Design: Skomsoy Gronlias.
Translation John Harley, Jorge Moniz, Francisco Garcia-Mora,
S. Engelschion, Luigi Spada, Nordis Redaktion, Siska Juul Andresen,
Berlitz translation services.